Passengers
of the
Titanic

Traveling on an
Ill–Fated Ship

by Sean Stewart Price

CONTENT CONSULTANT:

Captain Charles Weeks

Professor Emeritus in Marine Transportation

Maine Maritime Academy

CAPSTONE PRESS
a capstone imprint

Velocity Books are published by Capstone Press,
1710 Roe Crest Drive, North Mankato, Minnesota 56003
www.capstonepub.com

Library of Congress Cataloging-in-Publication Data
Cataloging-in-publication information is on file with the Library of Congress.
ISBN 978-1-4914-0421-8 (library binding)
ISBN 978-1-4914-0425-6 (ebook PDF)

Editorial Credits
Lauren Coss, editor; Craig Hinton, designer; Nikki Farinella, production specialist

Photo Credits
Alamy: Stephen Barnes, 14 (bottom), Zuma Press, Inc., 4 (bottom); Anonymous, 27; AP Images: Bebeto Matthews, 19 (middle), RMS Titanic Inc., 25; The Bridgeman Art Library: Bibliotheque Nationale, Paris, France/Archives Charmet, 36 (top); DK Images: Dorling Kindersley, 23; Library of Congress: 8 (right), 9 (all), 32 (top), 36 (bottom), 38, 40 (middle), 40 (bottom), 41 (right), Bain News Service, 8 (left); Maritime Quest, 6; National Geographic Creative: Raymond Wong, 30; Newscom: AFP/Getty Images, 34 (top), akg-images, 11, 32 (bottom), CB2/ZOB/wenn.com, 20 (top), Chris Melzer/ dpa/picture-alliance, 45 (bottom), Don Emmert/AFP/Getty Images, 14 (top), Everett Collection, 13, Gerry Penny/ EPA, 44, Lefranc David/ABACA, 10, 19 (top), Liam McArdle/Photoshot, 34 (bottom), Lionel Hahn KRT, 17 (bottom), Paramount/20th Century Fox, 45 (top), Shannon Wells Duncan/iPhoto Inc., 43 (top), Staff/Mirrorpix, 37, 41 (left), World History Archive, 22, 40 (top); North Wind Picture Archives, 12, 31, 35; Redline Editorial, 16 (map), 17 (map), 33 (map); Shutterstock Images: Joe Gough, 21 (bottom), Olinchuk, 20 (bottom), picturepartners, 21 (top), Sharon Eisenzopf, 42; SuperStock: Universal Images Group, 15, 19 (bottom), 39; Thinkstock: Dorling Kindersley, 28 (bottom), filo, 33 (ship icons), Ivan Mikhaylov, 20 (middle), Uros Petrovic, 26 (middle); Weldon Owen: Peter Bull Art Studio, 4–5, 24, Roger Stewart/KJA Artists, 26 (top), Wilkinson Studios/Francesca D'Ottav, cover

Artistic Effects
Shutterstock Images

Source Notes
Page 11 • Mahala Douglas, from "Affidavit of Mahala Douglas," from the United States Senate Inquiry, as published on *Titanic Inquiry Project.* http://www.titanicinquiry.org/USInq/AmInq15Douglas01.php; Page 12 • Amelia Brown, from a letter to her mother, published in "Miss Amelia Mary Brown," on *Encyclopedia Titanica.* org/titanic-survivor/mildred-brown.html; Page 15 • Marion Wright, quoted in *Shadow of the Titanic: The Extraordinary Stories of Those Who Survived,* by Andrew Wilson. New York: Atria Books, 2012. Page 16.; Page 22 • Lawrence Beesley, quoted in *Voyagers of the Titanic,* by Richard Davenport-Hines. New York: HarperCollins, 2012. Page 211.; Page 23 • Hugh Woolner, quoted in *Voyagers of the Titanic,* by Richard Davenport-Hines. New York: HarperCollins, 2012. Page 211.; Page 27 • Ida Straus, quoted in *Voyagers of the Titanic,* by Richard Davenport-Hines. New York: HarperCollins, 2012. Page 232.; Page 29 • Ruth Becker, quoted in *Titanic: Destination and Disaster: The Legends and the Reality,* by John P. Eaton. New York: Norton, 1987. Page 35.; Page 31 • John B. Thayer, Jr. "Thayer Describes Sinking of Titanic," as published in Philadelphia's *Evening Bulletin* on April 14, 1932. Courtesy of John Feeney. http://wormstedt.com/titanic/shots/thayer. html; Page 35 • Eva Hart, quoted in "Eva Miriam Hart," as published on *Encyclopedia Titanica.* http://www.encyclopedia-titanica.org/titanic-survivor/eva-hart.html; Page 41 • Robert Hichens, quoted in *Voyagers of the Titanic,* by Richard Davenport-Hines. New York: HarperCollins, 2012. Page 255.

Printed in the United States of America in North Mankato, Minnesota.
032015   008793R

Table of **Contents**

Traveling on *Titanic*

On April 10, 1912, the largest and most luxurious ocean liner built up to that time set sail from Southampton, England, bound for New York. The ship's name, *Titanic*, fit its enormous size. More than 1,300 passengers eagerly bought their tickets to travel on the grand ship. These passengers came from all over the world, from different social classes, and from all walks of life. Many saw traveling on *Titanic* as the trip of a lifetime.

Then on April 14, 1912, the unthinkable happened. *Titanic* scraped against an iceberg in the North Atlantic. Before long, it was clear the ship was sinking. All passengers faced life-or-death situations on the sinking ship. Meet a handful of *Titanic*'s passengers. Not all of them survived the disaster.

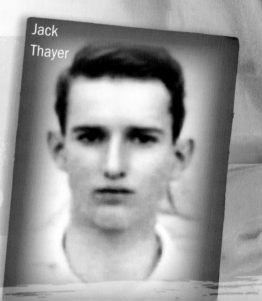

Jack Thayer

Jack Thayer, 17

Jack lived in Haverford, Pennsylvania. He and his parents were returning home on *Titanic* after a trip to Germany. They were traveling first class. On the night *Titanic* sank, Jack found himself stranded on the sinking ship with no more lifeboats available. How could he survive?

Ruth Becker, 12

Second-class passenger Ruth Becker was born in India to American parents who were Christian missionaries. But her brother's illness forced the family to return to the United States, where her brother could get better medical care. As *Titanic* went down, Ruth found herself separated from her family. Lifeboat space was running out. Should she look for her family or take a seat in a lifeboat while she had a chance?

Most passengers on *Titanic* believed the ship was unsinkable.

Banoura Ayoub, 14

Like most third-class passengers, Banoura was an immigrant. She was leaving Lebanon to join her uncle in Canada. She did not speak English. Banoura was traveling with three male cousins who were bound for Ohio. As *Titanic* sank, crew members were loading lifeboats with women and children only. Should Banoura stay with her cousins or seek safety without them?

Rossmore Abbott, 16

Rossmore was born in Rhode Island to an American father and a British mother. His parents separated in 1911. His mother, Rhoda, moved with him and his brother, Eugene, to Great Britain. Both Rossmore and Eugene became homesick for the United States, so Rhoda booked third-class passages for all three of them on *Titanic*. As the ship plunged into the freezing water, the Abbotts frantically looked for a chance of survival.

CHAPTER 1
The Voyage

APRIL 10, 1912

- *Titanic* picks up its first passengers in Southampton, England.

- *Titanic* picks up more passengers in Cherbourg, France.

APRIL 11, 1912

Titanic picks up its final passengers in Queenstown, Ireland, and sets sail for New York.

Titanic departs Southampton, England, on April 10, 1912.

FACT: In 1912 *Titanic* was the biggest vehicle built by humans to date. It was slightly larger than its two sister ships, *Olympic* and *Britannic*.

APRIL 18, 1912

Carpathia arrives in New York with *Titanic's* 712 survivors.

APRIL 15, 1912

- At approximately 2:20 a.m. *Titanic* sinks.

APRIL 14, 1912

Titanic hits an iceberg at about 11:40 p.m.

- *Carpathia* arrives and begins picking up *Titanic's* survivors at about 4:10 a.m.

The World of 1912

Titanic was built at a time when confidence was king. Over the course of just 100 years, technology had changed the way the world worked. The world of 1812 ran on wood fires, horses, and sailing ships. But the world of 1912, *Titanic's* world, ran on electric lights, cars, and giant steamships.

A company called White Star Line had *Titanic* built. White Star's officials wanted it to be the greatest steamship to ever set sail. The shipbuilding magazine *Shipbuilder* suggested *Titanic* was almost unsinkable. But in the minds of most passengers who boarded *Titanic* on April 10, 1912, it was just plain unsinkable.

White Star Line hoped to attract the wealthiest passengers to its great ship. But *Titanic* also included **accommodations** for passengers with less money. In 1912 much of society was divided into a system of three different social classes, an upper class, a middle class, and a lower class. Wealthy, upper-class people did not have much contact with middle-class people. Neither group had much contact with lower-class people, who were the poorest.

accommodation—a place where travelers can sleep, eat, and receive other services while traveling

7

Classes on *Titanic*

The price of a ticket on *Titanic* reflected a person's place in society. Like all ships of the time, *Titanic* kept the social classes separated.

Millionaire John Jacob Astor and his wife, Madeleine, were two of *Titanic*'s best-known first-class passengers. Madeleine survived the sinking. Her husband did not.

First Class

Number of passengers: 324

Ticket Price: up to $4,246 (about $100,000 in today's money)

★ People in first class were often millionaires who wanted only the finest accommodations and experiences onboard the ship. Many were wealthy industrialists traveling with their families. Others were British nobility. Some of the world's richest people sailed on *Titanic*.

FAMOUS FIRST-CLASS PASSENGERS

NAME	WHO WERE THEY?	FATE
John Jacob Astor	U.S. millionaire and businessman who financed the building of several fancy New York hotels	Died
Isidor and Ida Straus	Owners of Macy's department store	Died
Dorothy Gibson	Singer and silent-film actress	Survived
Jacques Futrelle	Mystery writer	Died
Lady Lucy Duff Gordon	Well-known fashion designer	Survived

Stuart Collett was a second-class passenger on Titanic who was studying to become a minister. He was emigrating from London, England, to New York, where much of his family lived. Collett survived the sinking in one of the ship's lifeboats.

Second Class

Number of passengers: 284

Ticket Price: $60 (about $1,400 in today's money)

★ These people were middle class. They included teachers, **clergymen**, engineers, and shopkeepers. Many were experienced travelers.

The Goldsmith family, Emily (*top left*), her husband, Frank (*top right*), and their son, Frankie (*bottom left*) traveled in third class aboard *Titanic*. Their youngest son, Bertie (*bottom right*), died in 1911, before the family made the journey. They were emigrating from England to Detroit, Michigan. Emily and Frankie survived the trip. Frank did not.

Third Class

Number of passengers: 709

Ticket Price: $15–$40 (about $350–$975 in today's money)

★ Most of *Titanic*'s third-class passengers were poor. Almost all of them were emigrants sailing to the United States to start a new life. Most had never sailed on a ship before.

clergyman—a minister, priest, rabbi, or other person appointed to perform religious work

Splendid Accommodations

Titanic's first-class section was built to be the world's fanciest hotel on water. Its centerpiece was the Grand Staircase. It was paneled in oak and included a giant skylight made of glass and wrought iron.

First-class rooms were located in the middle of the ship. This was where the boat's rocking was felt the least. All rooms were equipped with heaters, fans, and call bells for summoning stewards. Some rooms had telephones and private toilets. The rooms also had special lamps that stayed upright when seas became rough. People who had traveled first class on other ships marveled at how much more elegant *Titanic* was by comparison.

FACT: *Titanic's* first-class telephones could only communicate with other people on the ship. A telegraph system known as Marconi wireless was used to communicate with people onshore or on other ships.

> ❝ The boat was so luxurious, so steady, so immense, and such a marvel of a mechanism that one could not believe he was on a boat—and there the danger lay. We had smooth seas, clear, starlit nights, fresh favoring winds; nothing to mar our pleasure. ❞
>
> —First-class passenger Mahala Douglas

Titanic's first-class rooms, such as the one shown below, were designed to be as luxurious as the finest hotels of Europe and the United States.

telegraph—a machine that uses electrical signals to send messages over long distances

Some maids were responsible for caring for the children of wealthy people.

SECOND-CLASS SERVANTS

A few servants on *Titanic* traveled in second class. Of those who did, only one survived. She was 18-year-old Amelia Brown. Brown was the family cook for Canadian businessman Hudson Allison. She was in bed when *Titanic* hit the iceberg. At first Brown refused to get out of bed to find out what happened. "I couldn't believe that it was serious," she later wrote. A second-class passenger sharing Brown's room made her get up and get into a lifeboat. That act saved her life.

Servants on *Titanic*

First-class passengers on *Titanic* enjoyed traveling in style, which required servants. In all, about 43 personal servants accompanied their wealthy employers onboard *Titanic*. About 31 of them were personal maids and **valets**. There also were cooks, chauffeurs, clerks, secretaries, and **governesses**.

Some of the wealthiest travelers had several servants with them. For instance, John Jacob Astor had three servants: a valet, a maid for his wife, and a nurse. The nurse assisted Astor's wife, who was pregnant. Maids, valets, and nurses had very demanding jobs. They were expected to handle all of their employer's needs at any time of the day or night. For that reason, most servants traveled in first class.

Servants did not have an opportunity to enjoy most of *Titanic*'s first-class luxuries, such as the swimming pool and elegant dinners. However, they did stay in first-class rooms and had access to a servants' lounge. They could also enjoy walking outdoors on the **promenades**.

First-class servants were allowed to stroll down the same promenade as their employers.

valet—a person who attends to the personal needs of another person

governess—a woman who cares for and teaches a child in his or her home

promenade—a deck on a ship where passengers can stroll

WHITE STAR LINE
SOUTHAMPTON - CHERBOURG - NEW YORK
SECOND CLASS ★

NOT WANTED.

Second Class

The second-class rooms on *Titanic* were not as fancy as the first-class rooms. But they were so nice they would have been considered first-class rooms on any other ship. White Star Line planned to use some second-class cabins for first class if the regular first-class cabins filled to capacity.

A typical second-class room was furnished with a **mahogany** single bed or bunk bed and a matching wardrobe. The room also came with a comfortable sofa that could be converted into a bed. A foldaway washbasin cabinet doubled as a dresser. This provided more storage space. Unlike some first-class passengers, people in second class did not have their own toilets. They used restrooms down the hall from the cabins.

Second-class passengers ate in a private dining room. They also had access to a private promenade and a library.

a replica of a second-class cabin from *Titanic*

Second-class passengers
board *Titanic*.

66 **It is lovely on the water, except for the smell of new paint, everything is very comfortable on board.** 99

—Second-class passenger Marion Wright

mahogany—a dark, red-brown wood
often used in fine furniture

CANADA

UNITED STATES

PACIFIC OCEAN

ATLANTIC OCEAN

CUBA

MEXICO

PERU

URUGUAY

ARGENTINA

Third Class

Most of *Titanic*'s third-class rooms held two or four passengers. But some contained bunk beds for up to 10 passengers. The cabins were small, and they lacked decorations. But they were well lit and clean. Most passengers found the cabins quite comfortable.

Titanic's third-class passengers could enjoy meals prepared by the ship's staff in the third-class dining room. Third-class passengers also had a large hall where people could meet, talk, and play cards. Some third-class passengers were amateur musicians. Evenings in the third-class part of the ship were filled with singing and dancing.

Third-class passengers hoping for a breath of fresh air could stroll along the ship's bridge deck, near the back of the ship.

1. IRELAND
2. NORTHERN IRELAND
3. SCOTLAND
4. WALES
5. ENGLAND
6. CHANNEL ISLANDS
7. FRANCE
8. BELGIUM
9. NETHERLANDS
10. DENMARK
11. GERMANY
12. SWITZERLAND
13. AUSTRIA
14. HUNGARY
15. ITALY
16. SLOVENIA
17. CROATIA
18. BOSNIA
19. YUGOSLAVIA
20. BULGARIA
21. GREECE
22. SPAIN

A replica of one of *Titanic*'s third-class cabins is shown at an exhibit in California.

FACT: *Titanic* had only two bathtubs for the more than 700 third-class passengers aboard the ship. One was for women, and the other was for men. However, many people at the time believed taking frequent baths caused respiratory illnesses. So it is possible many passengers did not mind the lack of bathtubs.

Living in Luxury

Traveling across the Atlantic Ocean took about a week. People needed activities to keep them occupied. Most forms of recreation on the ship were reserved for first-class passengers.

★ They could work out in the ship's gymnasium, which was full of exercise equipment, including cycling and rowing machines. A crew member was on hand to help passengers as needed.

★ First-class passengers could take a dip in the saltwater swimming pool.

★ A **squash** court was available for passengers.

★ First-class passengers looking to relax could visit *Titanic*'s Turkish baths. This spa included a steam room, a hot room, a temperate room, a cooling room, and a shampooing room.

★ In the evenings after dinner, many men headed to the first-class smoking room. There they talked or played cards while enjoying pipes or cigars.

★ First-class women often spent time in the reading and writing room, where they could read and relax or compose letters or telegrams.

squash—a game played in an enclosed court in which two to four players hit a rubber ball with rackets

A crew member uses the rowing machine in *Titanic*'s gymnasium.

This chandelier from *Titanic*'s smoking room was recovered from the shipwreck site on the bottom of the ocean.

Titanic's reading and writing room

R.M.S. "TITANIC".

APRIL 10, 1912.

LUNCHEON.

CONSOMMÉ JARDINIERE   HODGE PODGE

FILLETS OF PLAICE

BEEF STEAK & KIDNEY PIE

ROAST SURREY CAPON

FROM THE GRILL.

GRILLED MUTTON CHOPS

MASHED, FRIED & BAKED JACKET POTATOES

RICE PUDDING

APPLES MANHATTAN   PASTRY

BUFFET.

FRESH LOBSTERS   POTTED SHRIMPS

SOUSED HERRINGS   SARDINES

ROAST BEEF

ROUND OF SPICED BEEF

VIRGINIA & CUMBERLAND HAM

BOLOGNA SAUSAGE   BRAWN

GALANTINE OF CHICKEN

CORNED OX TONGUE

LETTUCE   TOMATOES

CHEESE.

CHESHIRE, STILTON, GORGONZOLA, EDAM,

CAMEMBERT, ROQUEFORT, ST. IVEL.

Iced draught Munich Lager Beer 3d. & 6d. a Tankard.

Dining in Style

Food was a huge part of the *Titanic* experience. The ship's five kitchens rivaled the finest restaurants in Paris and London. Each of the three classes had different menus.

a first-class luncheon menu from *Titanic*

Sample of First-Class Menu Items

★ Raw oysters

★ Cream of barley soup

★ Poached Atlantic salmon with **mousseline sauce**

★ Lamb with mint sauce with boiled rice and green peas

★ Chocolate and vanilla **éclairs**

a sauce made from whipped cream and beaten eggs

a pastry that is filled with cream and topped with icing

Sample of Second-Class Menu Items

★ **Consommé** with tapioca

a type of flavorful soup

★ Baked **haddock**

a fish common in the North Atlantic

★ Plum pudding

Sample of Third-Class Menu Items

★ Rabbit pie

★ Baked potato

★ Bread and butter with rhubarb and ginger jam

Titanic Grocery List

Titanic carried enough food and drink to fill the 12,000 dinner plates and 8,000 glasses it had onboard. The foodstuffs included:

- 75,000 pounds (34,000 kilograms) of meat
- 40,000 eggs
- 25,000 pounds (11,300 kg) of poultry and game
- 11,000 pounds (5,000 kg) of fish
- 10,000 pounds (4,500 kg) of sugar

- 1,500 gallons (5,700 liters) of milk
- 438 gallons (1,660 l) of ice cream
- 40 tons (36 metric tons) of potatoes
- More than 1 ton (0.9 metric ton) of coffee

21

CHAPTER 2

Trouble for *Titanic*

an artist's rendition of *Titanic* colliding with an iceberg

66 There came what seemed to me nothing more than an extra heave of the engines and a more than usually obvious dancing motion of the mattress on which I sat. Nothing more than that. 99

—Second-class passenger Lawrence Beesley, from his cabin

> **We felt a rip that gave a sort of twist to the whole room.**
>
> —First-class passenger Hugh Woolner, from Titanic's first-class smoking room

The Engines Stop

For four days passengers on *Titanic* enjoyed an uneventful journey. Then at 11:40 p.m. on April 14, 1912, the great ship scraped the side of an iceberg. Passengers felt the impact differently, depending on where they were located on the ship. Some barely felt any movement at all. But passengers did notice when crew members stopped the engines a minute later.

Within half an hour of the crash, Captain Edward Smith and the ship's designer, Thomas Andrews, determined the ship was doomed. It had about two hours to stay afloat. Distress messages were sent to nearby ships. Within an hour, passengers saw crew members loading people into lifeboats.

Most passengers had no idea the great ship was in danger of sinking. A few young passengers even started a game of soccer with ice that had landed on the deck when *Titanic* scraped the iceberg.

WOMEN AND CHILDREN

Captain Smith ordered his officers to load women and children into the lifeboats. But some crew members followed the order differently. The officer loading boats on the starboard side allowed women and children to enter first. He allowed men onboard if no women were nearby. The officer on the port side understood the order to mean only women and children should enter the boats. As a result, many men were refused places in the boats. In some cases men were ordered off lifeboats despite the fact the boats had empty seats.

Fear and confusion filled *Titanic*'s lifeboats as crew members frantically lowered them into the icy water.

starboard—the right side of a ship looking forward

port—the left side of a ship looking forward

Boarding the lifeboats was not an easy task. First crew members uncovered the lifeboats and got the **davits** ready to lower the boats into the water. Then people had to step across a 2- to 3-foot (0.6- to 0.9-meter) gap between the ship and the swaying lifeboat. Anyone who missed took a five-story plunge into the water.

Hesitation

The first lifeboats were launched from *Titanic* at about 12:40 a.m. At first people did not want to get into the boats. It was a bitterly cold night. Few passengers wanted to leave the warmth of *Titanic*. Most people still believed *Titanic* was unsinkable.

Many passengers did not yet understand the lifeboats were their only chance of survival. As a result, crew members could not convince people to get into the boats. Each of the 14 wooden lifeboats was designed to hold 65 people. The first ones launched from *Titanic* were half empty.

A piece of a davit used to launch *Titanic*'s lifeboats can be seen at the shipwreck site.

davit—a small crane used on ships

Not Enough Lifeboats

By about 1:45 a.m., seawater flooding had reached the ship's upper decks. Now most people realized *Titanic* was sinking. Once that realization dawned, passengers soon found out what most of the crew already knew. The ship did not have enough lifeboats for everyone onboard. Some people remained calm and decided to stay with the ship. Many men stood aside to let more women and children into the lifeboats.

16   14   12   10

SECOND-CLASS PROMENADE

FUNNEL →

15   13   11   9

Ida Straus, the wife of Macy's department store owner Isidor Straus, had entered a lifeboat. But then she got out and decided to stay on *Titanic* with her husband. "We have been living together for many years," she told him, "and where you go, I go."

Most people, though, frantically looked for a way off *Titanic*. In some places people panicked and scrambled to get into the remaining lifeboats. People screamed and pushed to enter the few boats left.

Isidor and Ida Straus

Why Not More Lifeboats?

Titanic was certified to carry 3,547 people but had lifeboat capacity for only 1,178 people. However, the great ship actually had all the lifeboats required by law. Lawmakers of the time believed the number of safety features, such as lifeboats, should be decided by a ship's owners. Shipowners did not want more lifeboats. They cluttered the decks and left less room for promenades and other luxuries. Also many people really did think *Titanic* was unsinkable. If the huge ship started to sink, officials at White Star Line thought it would stay afloat long enough for help to arrive.

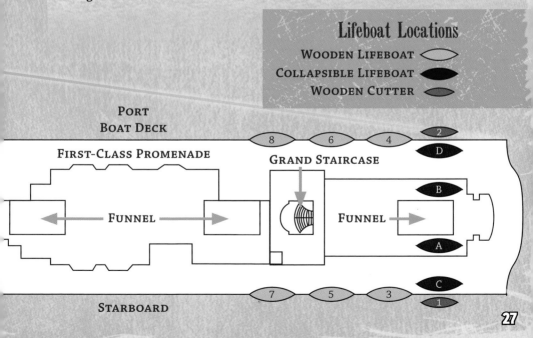

Lifeboat Locations

WOODEN LIFEBOAT

COLLAPSIBLE LIFEBOAT

WOODEN CUTTER

PORT
BOAT DECK

FIRST-CLASS PROMENADE

GRAND STAIRCASE

FUNNEL

FUNNEL

8 6 4 2

D

B

A

C

7 5 3 1

STARBOARD

Lifeboat Launch Times

LIFEBOAT #	LIFEBOAT TYPE	LAUNCH TIME
7	WOODEN	12:40 A.M.
5	WOODEN	12:45 A.M.
3	WOODEN	12:55 A.M.
8	WOODEN	1:00 A.M.
1	CUTTER	1:05 A.M.
6	WOODEN	1:10 A.M.
16	WOODEN	1:20 A.M.
14	WOODEN	1:25 A.M.
9	WOODEN	1:30 A.M.
12	WOODEN	1:30 A.M.
11	WOODEN	1:35 A.M.
13	WOODEN	1:40 A.M.
15	WOODEN	1:40 A.M.
2	CUTTER	1:45 A.M.
10	WOODEN	1:50 A.M.
4	WOODEN	1:50 A.M.
C	COLLAPSIBLE	2:00 A.M.
D	COLLAPSIBLE	2:05 A.M.
A	COLLAPSIBLE	2:15 A.M.*
B	COLLAPSIBLE	2:15 A.M.*

*Collapsible lifeboats A and B were never launched properly. They washed off the deck of *Titanic* as it sank. Some people survived by swimming to the overturned lifeboats and climbing on top of or hanging on to them.

Passengers began panicking as they put on their life vests and struggled to find a way off the ship.

Panic Spreads

In second class a steward had told Ruth Becker's family the ship was in an accident but would be on its way shortly. About 20 minutes later, the steward shouted for all hands on deck. Ruth became separated from her family when she returned to their room for blankets, but she remained calm and managed to get into a lifeboat.

At first third-class passenger Banoura Ayoub remained below deck with her cousins. Some first-class passengers came down and encouraged them to leave. Once on deck Banoura said good-bye to her three male cousins and was hustled into one of *Titanic*'s collapsible lifeboats.

Third-class passenger Rossmore Abbott and his family were unable to get into a lifeboat. They tried to stay on *Titanic* as long as possible. But all three family members were swept off the deck as seawater flooded onboard. The three swam to canvas lifeboat Collapsible A. It was full of water because it had not been launched properly. The boys helped their mother into the boat. Then they held onto the sides and waited.

> " Rowing away looking at the *Titanic*, it was a beautiful sight outlined against the starry sky, every porthole and saloon blazing with light. "
>
> —Second-class passenger Ruth Becker

FACT: The seawater around *Titanic* was about 28 degrees Fahrenheit (minus 2 degrees Celsius). At this temperature, most people in the water would die in less than 30 minutes.

CHAPTER 3

In the Water

An Icy Swim

By approximately 2:05 a.m., all but two collapsible lifeboats had been launched. Passengers still onboard *Titanic* faced limited options. The ship was sinking fast.

First-class passenger Jack Thayer became separated from his mother and father in the chaos on deck. Thayer debated what to do, finally deciding to swim for a boat. He jumped into the ice-cold water.

Gasping for breath, Thayer swam through a grim obstacle course. One of *Titanic*'s four funnels fell and landed about 10 yards (9 m) away. Thayer was freezing and exhausted by the time he reached an overturned boat. Along with 28 other soaking wet men who had climbed onto the boat, Thayer watched as *Titanic*'s rear section rose into the air. There was a massive crashing sound as the ship split in two.

Titanic split in half, and then its front section plunged toward the ocean floor.

Some of the men who survived the sinking took refuge on an overturned lifeboat.

66 The ship then corkscrewed around so that the propeller, rudder, and all seemed to go right over the heads of us on the upturned boat. Of course the lights now were all out. The ship seemed to hang in this position for minutes. Then with a dive and final plunge, the *Titanic* went under the water with very little apparent suction or noise. 99

—*First-class passenger Jack Thayer*

Survival

Once in the lifeboats, passengers had no choice but to wait for rescue. In their lifeboats Banoura Ayoub and Ruth Becker listened to the wails of mothers who had lost track of their children in the chaos.

The situation was more perilous for Jack Thayer and the 28 men on the overturned collapsible lifeboat B. One of the men, Harold Bride, worked as a wireless operator on *Titanic*. He told the men the ship *Carpathia* should reach them by around 4:00 a.m.

Rossmore Abbott and his brother, Eugene, clung to the edge of Collapsible A. Inside the boat, their mother, Rhoda, was too cold to speak. She watched helplessly as Eugene lost his grip and slipped into the Atlantic. Soon after Rossmore did the same.

While *Titanic*'s survivors waited in the lifeboats, *Carpathia*'s captain, Arthur Rostron, raced his ship toward the survivors.

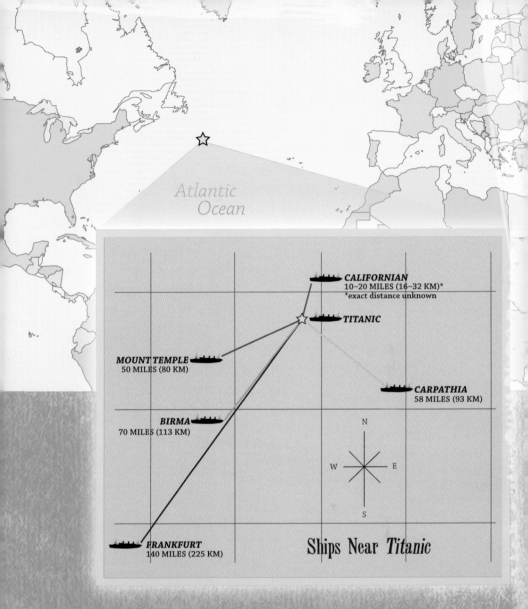

Atlantic
Ocean

CALIFORNIAN
10–20 MILES (16–32 KM)*
*exact distance unknown

TITANIC

MOUNT TEMPLE
50 MILES (80 KM)

CARPATHIA
58 MILES (93 KM)

BIRMA
70 MILES (113 KM)

N

W   E

S

FRANKFURT
140 MILES (225 KM)

Ships Near Titanic

FACT: The ship *Californian* was within 20 miles
(32 kilometers) of *Titanic* when the great ship
struck the iceberg. However, *Californian*'s wireless
operator had gone to bed when *Titanic*'s operators
sent the distress call. *Californian* did not receive
the message until it was too late.

A Handful of Lifeboats

Titanic sank at 2:20 a.m. on April 15. For survivors the half hour that followed the sinking was agonizing. Most of the more than 1,500 people who had not reached the lifeboats were alive in the water. But they were dying of **hypothermia**. They could survive no longer than a half hour in the freezing-cold water. Many died much sooner.

Titanic's life vests kept survivors afloat, but they offered no protection from the freezing water.

Frankie Goldsmith was nine years old when he survived *Titanic*'s sinking in one of the ship's collapsible lifeboats. He later compared the cries of the people in the water to the roar of a crowd at a baseball game.

Within 15 minutes the roar had mostly died down. Soon more than 1,500 people were dead in the water.

A replica of one of Titanic's wooden lifeboats can be seen in Belfast, Ireland.

one of *Titanic*'s collapsible lifeboats, loaded with passengers waiting for rescue

> 66 **There was nothing, just this deathly, terrible silence in the dark night with the stars overhead.** 99
>
> —*Eva Hart,*
> *seven-year-old survivor*

hypothermia—a life-threatening condition that occurs when a person's body temperature falls several degrees below normal

FACT: *Titanic* had several four-legged and winged passengers. There were 12 dogs, as well as several cats, chickens, and pet birds. Only three small lapdogs survived the sinking.

It was bitterly cold in the lifeboats as *Titanic's* passengers awaited rescue.

French brothers Michel (*left*) and Edmond (*right*) were only 4 and 2 when they survived the *Titanic* disaster in collapsible lifeboat D. Their father died in the sinking.

Harold Lowe (*left*), shown with Officer Charles Lightoller, was the only officer to return to pull survivors from the water.

A Long, Cold Night

The lifeboats held their own terrors. Many people had no idea when, or if, help would come. Few passengers were dressed for the bitterly cold night. Many were in thin nightclothes. Some were soaking wet, or their feet and legs were covered in standing water in the bottom of the boat. People cried, argued, sang religious hymns, and prayed.

Only one lifeboat went back to search for survivors. Like many others in the lifeboats, Officer Harold Lowe feared his boat would be swamped by going back to pick up survivors. So he waited until the survivors in the water stopped shouting. It was a fatal delay. By the time the boat returned, almost everyone was dead. Lowe pulled only four people from the water after *Titanic* sank. One died shortly after being brought aboard Lowe's lifeboat.

CHAPTER 4

The Aftermath

Titanic survivors
on Carpathia

Rescue!

Several ships heard *Titanic*'s distress call. One of the closest was *Carpathia*. It was 58 miles (93 km) from *Titanic*, which was more than four hours away. *Carpathia*'s captain, Arthur Rostron, had immediately turned his ship to help *Titanic*.

Carpathia arrived just after 4:00 a.m. It took another four hours to get everyone from the scattered lifeboats onboard *Carpathia*. The survivors were given food, blankets, and clothes. Doctors tended to the sick and wounded. The ship's crew and passengers gave up their own beds to *Titanic* survivors.

There were some happy moments for the 712 survivors. Ruth Becker was reunited with her mother, brother, and sister, who had been on a different lifeboat than her. But most passengers faced grief. Jack Thayer discovered his mother had survived, but his father had not. Almost everyone had a friend or loved one who died in the water.

Passengers on *Titanic*'s lifeboats are brought aboard *Carpathia*.

Heroes and Scapegoats

The news of *Titanic*'s sinking traveled quickly. People around the world were shocked and devastated by the disaster. Even before *Carpathia* reached New York on April 18, newspapers and government officials on both sides of the Atlantic began looking for heroes and **scapegoats**.

A London newspaper announces the *Titanic* tragedy.

TITANIC DISASTER GREAT LOSS OF LIFE EVENING NEWS

Heroes

ARTHUR ROSTRON

Carpathia's captain was widely praised for racing to the scene. His ship was too late to save most of *Titanic*'s passengers and crew. But Rostron did everything in his power to help.

Arthur Rostron

MARGARET BROWN

U.S. millionaire Margaret Brown became a popular figure. In the lifeboats, she helped row and keep spirits up. By the time *Carpathia* reached New York, Brown had raised almost $10,000 from first-class passengers to donate to poor survivors. She was later immortalized in a Broadway musical, *The Unsinkable Molly Brown*. But the play is mostly fictional.

Margaret "Molly" Brown

Scapegoats

J. Bruce Ismay

The president of the White Star Line was attacked in the press as soon as he arrived in New York. People wondered why he survived when so many other men died. They blamed him for the lack of lifeboats, even though no steamships at the time had enough lifeboats.

Stanley Lord

Lord was captain of *Californian*, the ship closest to *Titanic*'s location when it sank. *Californian* was no more than 20 miles (32 km) away from *Titanic*. Lord's crew witnessed the distress rockets fired by the sinking ship. But Lord felt his ship was trapped in a field of icebergs and should not move. He did little to investigate the situation.

Quartermaster Robert Hichens

On several lifeboats there were arguments about returning to save people in the water. Perhaps the biggest argument took place in Lifeboat 6. Margaret Brown and other passengers argued they should go back. They were overruled by Hichens, the crewman in charge of the boat. "It is our lives now, not theirs," he replied.

J. Bruce Ismay

Ismay is questioned by the U.S. Senate Committee after the disaster.

Stanley Lord

scapegoat—a person who is blamed for wrongdoing

41

Different Destinies

The people who survived *Titanic* went on to lead very different lives. Most struggled with troubling memories and the loss of loved ones. But their stories kept *Titanic*'s tale alive.

Jack Thayer became a successful banker and academic. For most of his life, he did not talk much about his time on *Titanic*. Later in life he wrote a pamphlet about his experiences in the sinking, which he printed for family and friends. Thayer died in 1945.

Like many other survivors, Ruth Becker did not talk about her experiences for decades. After she retired from her job as a teacher, she began attending *Titanic* conventions and discussing the sinking. She became a popular speaker. Becker died in 1990 at the age of 90.

Banoura Ayoub went to Canada to live with her uncle, but he refused to take her in because his son died in the sinking. Banoura married less than five months later. She raised the couple's seven children while her husband worked at automobile plants in the United States and Canada. She died in 1970.

A memorial in Washington, D.C., honors the men on *Titanic* who sacrificed themselves by allowing women and children into lifeboats.

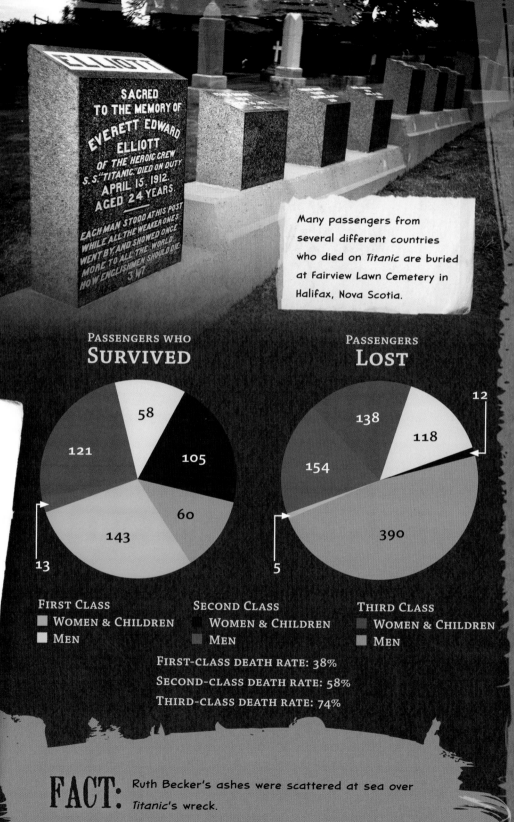

SACRED
TO THE MEMORY OF
EVERETT EDWARD
ELLIOTT
OF THE HEROIC CREW
S.S."TITANIC." DIED ON DUTY.
APRIL 15, 1912.
AGED 24 YEARS.

EACH MAN STOOD AT HIS POST
WHILE ALL THE WEAKER ONES
WENT BY, AND SHOWED ONCE
MORE TO ALL THE WORLD
HOW ENGLISHMEN SHOULD DIE.
3 W7

Many passengers from
several different countries
who died on *Titanic* are buried
at Fairview Lawn Cemetery in
Halifax, Nova Scotia.

PASSENGERS WHO
SURVIVED

58
121
105
60
143
13

PASSENGERS
LOST

12
138
118
154
390
5

FIRST CLASS
■ WOMEN & CHILDREN
■ MEN

SECOND CLASS
■ WOMEN & CHILDREN
■ MEN

THIRD CLASS
■ WOMEN & CHILDREN
■ MEN

FIRST-CLASS DEATH RATE: 38%
SECOND-CLASS DEATH RATE: 58%
THIRD-CLASS DEATH RATE: 74%

FACT: Ruth Becker's ashes were scattered at sea over
Titanic's wreck.

The Last Survivors

After April 15, 1912, people around the world built memorials to *Titanic*'s victims. Many people wrote books and made movies about the disaster. But as survivors and those who lost loved ones gradually died, interest in *Titanic* faded.

Then in the late 1900s, events reignited people's curiosity about the tragedy. In 1985 oceanographer Robert Ballard discovered the ship's long-lost wreck. This prompted journalists to seek out survivors so they could retell their stories. In 1997 the blockbuster movie *Titanic* made the tragedy fresh for a new generation of people. In 2012 the 100th anniversary of the disaster also generated new interest in *Titanic*.

Millvina Dean was the last living survivor of the *Titanic* disaster. Dean was only nine weeks old at the time of the sinking. She did not even know she had been on *Titanic* until she was eight years old. But Dean knew her family's memories of the sinking and shared their stories. She died in 2009 at the age of 97. She and other survivors have ensured *Titanic*'s story will never be forgotten.

Millvina Dean

The 1997 film *Titanic*, starring actors Leonardo DiCaprio and Kate Winslet, renewed interest in the ship.

A SPECIAL GIFT

In 1993 *Titanic* survivor Edith Haisman was presented with her father's gold pocket watch. She last saw the watch at age 15 when she said good-bye to her father on *Titanic*'s deck. He went down with the ship. A company collecting artifacts from *Titanic*'s wreck found his watch.

Ballard explains a picture of *Titanic*'s upper-deck wreckage.

Glossary

accommodation (uh-kah-muh-DAY-shuhn)—a place where travelers can sleep, eat, and receive other services while traveling

clergyman (KLUR-jee-man)—a minister, priest, rabbi, or other person appointed to perform religious work

davit (DAHV-it)—a small crane used on ships

governess (GUH-vur-nuss)—a woman who cares for and teaches a child in his or her home

hypothermia (hye-puh-THUR-mee-uh)—a life-threatening condition that occurs when a person's body temperature falls several degrees below normal

mahogany (muh-HAH-guh-nee)—a dark, red-brown wood often used in fine furniture

port (PORT)—the left side of a ship looking forward

promenade (prah-muh-NADE)—a deck on a ship where passengers can stroll

scapegoat (SKAPE-goht)—a person who is blamed for wrongdoing

squash (SKWAHSH)—a game played in an enclosed court in which two to four players hit a rubber ball with rackets

starboard (STAR-burd)—the right side of a ship looking forward

telegraph (TEL-uh-graf)—a machine that uses electrical signals to send messages over long distances

valet (va-LAY)—a person who attends to the personal needs of another person

Read More

Burgan, Michael. Titanic: *Truth and Rumors*. Truth and Rumors. Mankato, Minn.: Capstone Press, 2010.

Hopkinson, Deborah. Titanic: *Voices from the Disaster*. New York: Scholastic Press, 2012.

Noon, Steve. *Story of the* Titanic. New York: DK, 2012.

Critical Thinking Using the Common Core

1. This book describes the experiences of four different passengers from the three different classes on *Titanic*. How did these four passengers experience the sinking differently? How were their experiences the same? Use specific examples from the text. (Key Ideas and Details)

2. As *Titanic* was sinking, many of its lifeboats launched were not full. What do you think are some of the reasons for this? Use the text from pages 24 and 27 to support your answer. (Key Ideas and Details)

3. The charts on page 43 show the survival statistics for different passengers. What does this tell you about which genders and classes were most likely to survive? More third-class men were lost than any other group. Why might this be the case? (Craft and Structure)

Internet Sites

FactHound offers a safe, fun way to find Internet sites related to this book. All of the sites on FactHound have been researched by our staff.

Here's all you do:

Visit *www.facthound.com*

Type in this code: 9781491404218

Index